W9-AUY-053

Favorite Brand Name™

Publications International, Ltd.

Favorite Brand Name Recipes at www.fbnr.com

Copyright © 2007 Publications International, Ltd.
All rights reserved. This publication may not be reproduced or quoted in whole or in part by any means whatsoever without written permission from:

Louis Weber, CEO
Publications International, Ltd.
7373 North Cicero Avenue
Lincolnwood, IL 60712

Permission is never granted for commercial purposes.

Favorite Brand Name is a trademark of Publications International, Ltd.

All recipes and photographs that contain specific brand names are copyrighted by those companies and/or associations, unless otherwise specified. All photographs *except* that on page 9 copyright © Publications International, Ltd.

Glad® is a registered trademark of The Glad Products Company.

Some of the products listed in this publication may be in limited distribution.

Pictured on the front cover *(top to bottom):* Miss Pinky the Pig Cupcake *(page 86)* and Breakfast Mice *(page 52).*

Pictured on the back cover *(left to right):* Veggie Wedgies *(page 26)* and Banana Roll-Ups *(page 4).*

ISBN-13: 978-1-4127-2906-2
ISBN-10: 1-4127-2906-8

Manufactured in China.

8 7 6 5 4 3 2 1

Microwave Cooking: Microwave ovens vary in wattage. Use the cooking times as guidelines and check for doneness before adding more time.

Preparation/Cooking Times: Preparation times are based on the approximate amount of time required to assemble the recipe before cooking, baking, chilling or serving. These times include preparation steps such as measuring, chopping and mixing. The fact that some preparations and cooking can be done simultaneously is taken into account. Preparation of optional ingredients and serving suggestions is not included.

Contents

Fruit Fun

banana roll-ups

¼ cup smooth or crunchy almond butter
2 tablespoons mini chocolate chips
1 to 2 tablespoons milk
1 (8-inch) whole wheat flour tortilla
1 large banana, peeled

1. Combine almond butter, chocolate chips and 1 tablespoon milk in medium microwavable bowl. Microwave on MEDIUM (50%) 40 seconds. Stir well and repeat if necessary to melt chocolate. Add more milk if necessary for desired consistency.

2. Spread almond butter mixture on tortilla. Place banana on one side of tortilla and roll up tightly. Cut into 8 slices.

Makes 4 servings

helpful hint

Take advantage of some of the wonderful new flavors and colors of tortillas that are available today. You can create colorful roll-ups with a red (tomato) or green (spinach) tortilla and contrasting fillings.

green meanies

4 green apples
1 cup nut butter (cashew, almond or peanut butter)
Almond slivers

1. Place apple, stem side up, on cutting board. Cut away 2 halves from sides of apple, leaving 1-inch-thick center slice with stem and core. Discard core slice. Cut each half round in half. Then cut each apple quarter into two wedges using crinkle cutter. Repeat with remaining apples. Each apple will yield 8 wedges.

2. Spread 2 teaspoons nut butter on wide edge of apple slice. Top with another apple slice, aligning crinkled edges to resemble jaws. Insert almond slivers to make fangs. *Makes 8 servings*

easy raspberry ice cream

1³/₄ cups frozen unsweetened raspberries
2 to 3 tablespoons powdered sugar
¹/₂ cup whipping cream

1. Place raspberries in food processor fitted with steel blade. Process using on/off pulses about 15 seconds or until raspberries resemble coarse crumbs.

2. Add sugar; process using on/off pulses until smooth. With processor running, add cream; process until well blended. Serve immediately. *Makes 3 servings*

variation: Substitute other fruits such as strawberries for the raspberries.

watermelon banana split

2 bananas
1 medium watermelon
1 cup fresh blueberries
1 cup diced fresh pineapple
1 cup sliced fresh strawberries
¼ cup caramel fruit dip
¼ cup honey roasted almonds

Peel bananas and cut in half lengthwise then cut each piece in half.
For each serving, lay 2 banana pieces against sides of shallow dish.
Using an ice cream scooper, place three watermelon "scoops" in
between each banana in each dish. Remove seeds if necessary. Top
each watermelon "scoop" with a different fresh fruit topping. Drizzle
caramel fruit dip over all. Sprinkle with almonds.   *Makes 4 servings*

Favorite recipe from **National Watermelon Promotion Board**

helpful hint

*Most children love watermelon, so why not serve it for dessert
more often? These days watermelon comes in traditional red, plus
pink or yellow. You don't need to buy a whole watermelon either.
Choose a pre-cut slice that is well wrapped. It should be firm,
juicy and brightly colored, not grainy or dried out.*

sweet 'n' easy fruit crisp bowls

2 tablespoons low-fat granola with almonds
Nonstick cooking spray
1 large red apple, such as Gala, cut into ¹/₂-inch pieces
1 tablespoon dried sweetened cranberries
¹/₄ teaspoon apple pie spice or ground cinnamon
1 teaspoon butter
1 packet sugar substitute
¹/₄ teaspoon almond extract
2 tablespoons low-fat vanilla ice cream

1. Place granola in small resealable food storage bag and crush lightly to form a coarse meal. Set aside.

2. Heat large skillet over medium heat; coat with cooking spray. Add apples, cranberries and apple pie spice. Cook 4 minutes or until apples are just tender, stirring frequently. Remove from heat; stir in butter, sugar substitute and almond extract. Spoon onto 2 dessert plates. Sprinkle with granola and top with ice cream. Serve immediately. *Makes 2 servings*

note: You can make apple mixture up to 8 hours in advance and top with granola and ice cream at time of serving. To warm crisp, microwave apple mixture (before adding granola and ice cream) 20 to 30 seconds on HIGH or until slightly heated.

strawberry-topped waffles with sweet and creamy sauce

Prep Time: 10 minutes

> 3 ounces reduced-fat cream cheese
> 1/4 cup fat-free half-and-half
> 3 packets sugar substitute
> 1/4 teaspoon vanilla
> 4 frozen waffles
> 1 1/3 cup sliced fresh strawberries

1. Combine cream cheese, half-and-half, sugar substitute and vanilla in blender; blend until smooth.

2. Toast waffles. Spoon sauce over waffles; top with strawberries.

Makes 4 servings

apple cinnamon chunkies

> 1 package (18 ounces) refrigerated oatmeal raisin cookie dough
> 1 cup chopped dried apples
> 1/2 cup cinnamon baking chips
> 1/2 teaspoon apple pie spice*

Substitute 1/4 teaspoon ground cinnamon, 1/8 teaspoon ground nutmeg and pinch of ground allspice or ground cloves for 1/2 teaspoon apple pie spice.

1. Preheat oven to 350°F. Lightly grease cookie sheets. Let dough stand at room temperature about 15 minutes.

2. Combine dough, apples, cinnamon chips and apple pie spice in large bowl; stir until well blended. Drop dough by rounded tablespoonfuls 2 inches apart onto prepared cookie sheets.

3. Bake 10 to 12 minutes or until golden brown. Cool on cookie sheets 2 to 3 minutes. Remove to wire racks; cool completely.

Makes 2 dozen cookies

banana freezer pops

  2 ripe medium bananas
  1 can (6 ounces) frozen orange juice concentrate
¼ cup water
  1 tablespoon honey
  1 teaspoon vanilla
  8 (3-ounce) paper or plastic cups
  8 wooden sticks

1. Peel bananas; break into chunks. Place in food processor or blender.

2. Add orange juice concentrate, water, honey and vanilla; process until smooth.

3. Pour banana mixture evenly into cups. Cover top of each cup with small piece of aluminum foil. Insert wooden stick through center of foil into banana mixture.

4. Place cups on tray; freeze until firm, about 3 hours. To serve, remove foil and tear off paper cups (or slide out of plastic cups).

Makes 8 servings

peppy purple pops: Omit honey and vanilla. Substitute grape juice concentrate for orange juice concentrate.

frozen banana shakes: Increase water to 1½ cups. Prepare fruit mixture as directed. Add 4 ice cubes; process on high speed until mixture is thick and creamy. Makes 3 servings.

banana caterpillars

2 medium bananas
¼ cup peanut butter
¼ cup sweetened flaked coconut
4 raisins
6 thin pretzel sticks

1. Peel and slice each banana into 10 segments. Assemble caterpillar by spreading segments with peanut butter, pressing pieces together.

2. Sprinkle half of flaked coconut over each caterpillar and press lightly with fingertips to coat. Press 2 raisins on 1 end to form eyes using additional peanut butter to adhere.

3. Break pretzel sticks into small pieces and press into peanut butter for legs and antennae.

Makes 2 servings

helpful hint

Kids can also be creative and add other types of sliced fruits (strawberries, apples, pears) to their caterpillars.

frozen chocolate-covered bananas

2 ripe medium bananas
4 wooden sticks
$\frac{1}{2}$ cup low-fat granola cereal without raisins
$\frac{1}{3}$ cup hot fudge topping, at room temperature

1. Line baking sheet with waxed paper; set aside.

2. Peel bananas; cut each in half crosswise. Insert wooden stick into center of cut end of each banana about $1\frac{1}{2}$ inches into banana half. Place on prepared baking sheet; freeze until firm, at least 2 hours.

3. Place granola in large food storage bag; crush slightly using rolling pin or meat mallet. Transfer granola to shallow plate. Place hot fudge topping in shallow dish.

4. Working with 1 banana at a time, place frozen banana in hot fudge topping; turn banana and spread topping evenly onto banana with small rubber scraper. Immediately place banana on plate with granola; turn to coat lightly. Return to baking sheet in freezer. Repeat with remaining bananas.

5. Freeze until hot fudge topping is very firm, at least 2 hours. Place on small plates; let stand 5 minutes before serving.

Makes 4 servings

taffy apple bars

1 package (18 ounces) refrigerated sugar cookie dough
1 package (18 ounces) refrigerated peanut butter
    cookie dough
½ cup all-purpose flour
2 large apples, cored, peeled and chopped (3½ to 4 cups)
1 cup chopped peanuts
½ cup caramel ice cream topping

1. Preheat oven to 350°F. Lightly grease 13×9-inch baking pan. Let both packages of dough stand at room temperature about 15 minutes.

2. Combine both doughs and flour in large bowl; beat until well blended. Press dough evenly onto bottom of prepared pan. Spoon apples evenly over dough; press down lightly. Sprinkle with peanuts.

3. Bake about 35 minutes or until edges are brown and center is set. Cool completely in pan on wire rack. Drizzle with caramel topping.

Makes about 2 dozen bars

jiggly banana split

Prep Time: 5 minutes

1 banana
3 gelatin snack cups (3 ounces each), any flavors
2 tablespoons whipped topping
    Colored sprinkles
1 maraschino cherry

1. Peel banana and cut in half lengthwise. Place banana in serving dish, separating slices. Unmold gelatin snack cups by dipping partially in warm water for a few seconds. Slide gelatin from cups; place between banana slices.

2. Top with dollops of whipped topping, sprinkles and cherry.

Makes 1 serving

Veggie Magic

salmon celery trees

    1 can (6 ounces) pink salmon
    2 tablespoons minced fresh dill
    1 tablespoon minced green onion (optional)
    1 tablespoon fresh lemon juice
    6 ounces cream cheese, softened
      Salt and black pepper
   12 celery stalks
      Fresh dill sprigs, 3 to 4 inches long

1. Combine salmon, dill, onion, if desired, and lemon juice in medium bowl. Mix until well combined. Add cream cheese and mash with fork until mixture is smooth. Season to taste with salt and pepper.

2. Stack celery stalks in pairs. Cut each pair into 3-inch pieces.

3. Spread 2 tablespoons salmon mixture into hollowed section of celery. Press dill springs into one half of each celery pair before pressing filled sides together. Stand upright on serving platter.

Makes 12 servings

kids' oasis

HUMMUS

2 cans (15 ounces each) chickpeas, rinsed and drained
¼ cup tahini (sesame paste)
   Juice from 1 lemon
1 tablespoon olive oil
3 cloves garlic, minced
½ teaspoon salt
¼ teaspoon ground black pepper

BROCCOLI "TREES" AND COUSCOUS "SAND"

2 cups broccoli florets
1 box (10 ounces) couscous, plus ingredients to prepare
   couscous
   Green onions and chives (optional)

1. To make hummus, place chickpeas, tahini, lemon juice, oil, garlic, salt and pepper in food processor. Process 2 to 3 minutes or until coarse paste is formed, stopping processor and scraping side of bowl occasionally. Set aside.

2. Cook broccoli florets in boiling salted water until crisp-tender; drain and set aside.

3. Meanwhile, prepare couscous according to package directions. To make each oasis, spread ¼ cup hummus in center of plate. Insert broccoli "trees" and surround with couscous "sand." Drizzle with additional olive oil and garnish with green onions and chives, if desired. Serve with pita bread.   *Makes about 12 servings*

cheesy barbecued bean dip

    ½ cup canned vegetarian baked beans
    3 tablespoons pasteurized process cheese spread
    2 tablespoons regular or hickory smoke barbecue sauce
    2 large carrots, cut into diagonal slices
    1 medium red or green bell pepper, cut into chunks

MICROWAVE DIRECTIONS

1. Place beans in small microwavable bowl; mash slightly with fork. Stir in process cheese spread and barbecue sauce. Cover with vented plastic wrap.

2. Microwave on HIGH 1 minute; stir. Microwave 30 seconds or until hot. Serve with carrot slices and bell pepper chunks.

Makes 4 servings

cheesy potato cups

    4 (6-ounce) baking potatoes, pierced with fork
    ⅓ cup fat-free (skim) milk
    1 tablespoon butter
    ¼ teaspoon salt
    2 ounces American cheese, cut in 8 cubes
    8 broccoli florets

MICROWAVE DIRECTIONS

Microwave potatoes on HIGH 10 minutes. When cool enough to handle, slice in half crosswise to make cup shapes. Trim bottoms so potatoes sit upright. Scoop out centers into medium bowl. Mash potatoes; beat in milk, butter and salt until blended. Stuff potato cups and arrange in microwavable dish. Top each with cheese cube and broccoli floret. Microwave 2 minutes or until cheese melts.

Makes 4 servings

oven "fries"

2 small baking potatoes
2 teaspoons olive oil
¼ teaspoon salt or onion salt

1. Place potatoes in refrigerator for 1 to 2 days.

2. Preheat oven to 450°F. Peel potatoes and cut lengthwise into ¼-inch square strips. Place in colander. Rinse potato strips under cold running water 2 minutes. Drain. Pat dry with paper towels. Place potatoes in small resealable food storage bag. Drizzle with oil. Seal bag; shake to coat potatoes with oil.

3. Arrange potatoes in single layer on baking sheet. Bake 20 to 25 minutes or until light brown and crisp. Sprinkle with salt or onion salt.   *Makes 2 servings*

note: Refrigerating potatoes—usually not recommended—converts starch in the potatoes to sugar, which enhances the browning when the potatoes are baked. Do not refrigerate the potatoes longer than 2 days or they may begin to taste sweet.

microwave sweet potato chips

2 cups thinly sliced sweet potatoes
1 tablespoon packed brown sugar
2 teaspoons margarine

MICROWAVE DIRECTIONS

Place sweet potatoes in single layer in microwavable dish. Sprinkle with water. Microwave at HIGH 5 minutes. Stir in brown sugar and margarine. Microwave at HIGH 2 to 3 minutes. Let stand a few minutes before serving.   *Makes 4 servings*

*Favorite recipe from **The Sugar Association, Inc.***

veggie wedgies

Prep Time: 10 minutes • Cook Time: 13 minutes

2 tablespoons olive oil
1 small onion, thinly sliced
1 small red bell pepper, thinly sliced
1 jar (1 pound 10 ounces) RAGÚ® Organic Pasta Sauce, divided
4 (10-inch) burrito-size flour tortillas
1 cup shredded mozzarella cheese (about 4 ounces)

In 12-inch nonstick skillet, heat 1 tablespoon olive oil over medium-high heat and cook onion and red pepper, stirring occasionally, 4 minutes or until softened. Reduce heat to medium, then stir in 1½ cups Pasta Sauce. Simmer, stirring occasionally, 5 minutes or until sauce is thickened. Evenly spread sauce mixture on tortillas, leaving a 1-inch border. Then top with cheese and fold in half; set aside. Clean skillet.

In same skillet, heat remaining 1 tablespoon olive oil over medium heat and cook quesadillas, 2 at a time, turning once, 4 minutes or until golden brown and cheese is melted. Cut quesadillas into wedges and serve with remaining Pasta Sauce, heated.   *Makes 4 servings*

variation: Quesadillas can also be baked. Place folded filled tortillas on baking sheet and bake in preheated 425°F oven 5 minutes or until cheese is melted. Cut and serve as above.

helpful hint

Quesadillas are a popular Mexican snack that are a hit with kids here, too. They're versatile and great finger food. Try creating special combinations based on your family's food preferences. Almost any combination of vegetable, meat and cheese works well. Quesadillas are also a delicious way to use up leftovers.

abc slaw

　　2 green apples, cut into thin strips
　　1 package (10 ounces) broccoli slaw with carrots
　　3 stalks celery, cut into thin slices
　　1 fennel bulb, cut into thin strips
　　$1/4$ cup creamy salad dressing
　　1 tablespoon lemon juice
　　$1/2$ teaspoon red pepper flakes

Combine all ingredients in large bowl; mix well. Chill 1 hour before serving.

Makes 4 to 6 servings

cherry tomato planets

　　1 bag (20 ounces) cherry tomatoes (about 20)
　　$1/4$ cup (1 ounce) shredded mozzarella cheese
　　20 slices pepperoni

1. Preheat broiler. Slice upper $1/8$ inch off stem end of tomatoes; reserve tops. Core tomatoes using small melon baller or spoon.

2. Fill each tomato with cheese, top with slice of pepperoni, and cover with tomato top. Secure with toothpick.

3. Place filled tomatoes on baking sheet. Broil 6 inches from heat 3 minutes or until cheese is melted and tomatoes just begin to shrivel.

4. Transfer tomatoes to paper towel-lined plate to drain. Remove toothpicks before serving. Serve warm (not hot).

Makes about 20 appetizers

cheddar broccoli martians

Prep Time: 25 minutes • Cook Time: 10 minutes

1 package (10 ounces) frozen chopped broccoli, thawed
1 jar (1 pound) RAGÚ® Cheesy! Double Cheddar Sauce
2 tablespoons Italian seasoned dry bread crumbs
1 package (12 ounces) refrigerated flaky buttermilk biscuits
    (10 biscuits)
    Green food coloring
1 egg
    Martian Garnishes*

*For Martian Garnishes, use thinly sliced carrot rounds and peas for eyes, broccoli for nose and eyebrows and chow mein noodles for antenna and mouth.

Preheat oven to 400°F. Arrange broccoli on double layer of paper towels and squeeze dry. In small bowl, combine broccoli, ³/₄ cup Double Cheddar Sauce and bread crumbs; set aside.

Separate biscuits in half to make 20 pieces. On lightly floured surface, roll each into a 3¹/₂-inch circle. On ungreased baking sheet, arrange 10 biscuit circles. Evenly spread 10 circles with broccoli mixture leaving ¹/₂-inch border. Top with remaining biscuit circles, sealing edges tightly with fork. Beat 4 drops food coloring with egg, then brush on circles.

Bake 10 minutes or until golden. Serve with remaining Double Cheddar Sauce, heated.   *Makes 10 servings*

sweet & tangy marinated vegetables

8 cups mixed fresh vegetables, such as broccoli, cauliflower, zucchini, carrots and red bell peppers, cut into 1- to 1¹/₂-inch pieces

¹/₃ cup distilled white vinegar

¹/₄ cup sugar

¹/₄ cup water

1 packet (1 ounce) HIDDEN VALLEY® The Original Ranch® Salad Dressing & Seasoning Mix

Place vegetables in a gallon-size Glad® Zipper Storage Bag. Combine vinegar, sugar, water and salad dressing & seasoning mix in a medium bowl. Whisk until sugar dissolves; pour over vegetables. Seal bag and shake to coat. Refrigerate 4 hours or overnight, turning bag occasionally. *Makes 8 servings*

note: Vegetables will keep up to 3 days in refrigerator.

helpful hint

When you're in a hurry, pick up a variety of vegetables from the salad bar at your local market. Sure, it's more expensive, but you can choose a wide variety of produce that's ready to go and save yourself preparation, washing and trimming time.

blt cukes

3 slices crisp-cooked bacon, chopped
¹⁄₂ cup finely chopped lettuce
¹⁄₂ cup finely chopped baby spinach
¹⁄₄ cup diced tomato
1¹⁄₂ tablespoons mayonnaise
Pinch salt
¹⁄₄ teaspoon black pepper
1 large cucumber
Minced parsley or green onion (optional)

1. Combine bacon, lettuce, spinach, tomato and mayonnaise. Season with salt and pepper; set aside.

2. Peel cucumber. Trim off ends and slice in half lengthwise. Use spoon to scoop out seeds; discard seeds. Divide BLT mixture between cucumber halves, mounding in hollowed areas. Garnish with parsley. Cut into 2-inch pieces. *Makes 8 to 10 pieces*

note: Make these snacks when cucumbers are plentiful and large enough to easily hollow out with a spoon. You may make these up to 12 hours ahead of time and chill until serving.

great zukes pizza bites

1 medium zucchini
3 tablespoons pizza sauce
2 tablespoons tomato paste
¼ teaspoon dried oregano leaves
¾ cup (3 ounces) shredded reduced-fat mozzarella cheese
¼ cup shredded Parmesan cheese
8 slices pitted ripe olives
8 slices pepperoni

1. Preheat broiler; set rack 4 inches from heat.

2. Trim off and discard end of zucchini. Cut zucchini into 16 (¼-inch-thick) diagonal slices. Place zucchini on nonstick baking sheet.

3. Combine pizza sauce, tomato paste and oregano in small bowl until well blended. Spread scant teaspoon sauce over each zucchini slice. Combine mozzarella and Parmesan cheeses in small bowl. Top each zucchini slice with 1 tablespoon cheese mixture, pressing down into sauce. Place 1 olive slice on each of 8 pizza bites. Place 1 folded pepperoni slice on each remaining pizza bite.

4. Broil 3 minutes or until cheese is melted and zucchini is tender. Serve immediately. *Makes 8 servings*

Finger Food

focaccia bars

　　Cornmeal
　1 package (about 11 ounces) refrigerated French bread dough
　2 tablespoons olive oil
　1 large yellow or red bell pepper, cored and thinly sliced
　1/4 teaspoon coarse salt
　1/8 teaspoon dried oregano
　3 tablespoons shredded Italian cheese blend

1. Preheat oven to 400°F. Sprinkle cornmeal on baking sheet. Unwrap bread dough and shape into 16×4-inch strip on prepared baking sheet. Set aside.

2. Heat olive oil in medium skillet over medium-high heat. Add bell pepper; cook and stir 3 to 5 minutes or until pepper is tender and lightly browned. Remove; reserve oil.

3. Press fingertips into dough to create dimples. Drizzle leftover cooking oil from skillet onto dough. Spread pepper slices over dough. Sprinkle with salt and oregano. Top with cheese.

4. Bake 13 to 15 minutes or until cheese melts and bread is firm and golden. Let focaccia rest 2 to 3 minutes. Cut into 4 (4-inch) bars. Serve warm or at room temperature. *Makes 4 servings*

note: Refrigerate leftovers up to two days or freeze up to one month.

tortellini teasers

Zesty Tomato Sauce (recipe follows)
$\frac{1}{2}$ (9-ounce) package refrigerated cheese tortellini
1 large red or green bell pepper, cut into 1-inch pieces
2 medium carrots, cut into $\frac{1}{2}$-inch pieces
1 medium zucchini, cut into $\frac{1}{2}$-inch pieces
12 medium fresh mushrooms
12 cherry tomatoes

1. Prepare Zesty Tomato Sauce; keep warm.

2. Cook tortellini according to package directions; drain.

3. Alternate 1 tortellini and 2 to 3 vegetable pieces on long frilled toothpicks or wooden skewers. Serve as dippers with tomato sauce.

Makes 6 servings

zesty tomato sauce

1 can (15 ounces) tomato purée
2 tablespoons finely chopped onion
2 tablespoons chopped fresh parsley
1 teaspoon dried oregano
$\frac{1}{4}$ teaspoon dried thyme
$\frac{1}{4}$ teaspoon salt
$\frac{1}{8}$ teaspoon black pepper

Combine tomato purée, onion, parsley, oregano and thyme in small saucepan. Heat thoroughly, stirring occasionally. Stir in salt and pepper. Garnish with carrot curl, if desired.

peanut butter-apple wraps

Prep Time: 5 minutes • Chill Time: 2 hours

> ³/₄ **cup creamy peanut butter**
> 4 **(7-inch) whole wheat or spinach tortillas**
> ³/₄ **cup finely chopped apple**
> ¹/₃ **cup shredded carrot**
> ¹/₃ **cup low-fat granola without raisins**
> 1 **tablespoon toasted wheat germ**

Spread peanut butter on one side of each tortilla. Sprinkle each tortilla evenly with apple, carrot, granola and wheat germ. Roll up tightly. Cut each roll in half and secure with toothpick. Serve immediately or refrigerate until ready to serve.   *Makes 4 servings*

peachy sunflower

> 6 **ounces low-fat vanilla yogurt**
> ¹/₄ **cup peach jam**
> **Pinch ground ginger (optional)**
> 2 **to 3 drops yellow food coloring**
> ¹/₃ **cup semisweet chocolate chips**
> 16 **to 20 gingersnap cookies**

1. Mix yogurt, jam and ginger, if desired, in small bowl. Mix in food coloring until evenly blended.

2. Spread yogurt mixture in small bowl and dot top with chocolate chips. Place small bowl on top of larger serving plate or tray, and arrange gingersnaps in a circle around edge. Overlap cookie edges to look like petals.   *Makes 8 to 10 servings*

maraschino-lemonade pops

1 (10-ounce) jar maraschino cherries

8 (3-ounce) paper cups

1 (12-ounce) can frozen pink lemonade concentrate, partly
   thawed

¼ cup water

8 popsicle sticks

Drain cherries, reserving juice. Place one whole cherry in each paper cup. Coarsely chop remaining cherries. Add chopped cherries, lemonade concentrate, water and reserved juice to container of blender or food processor; blend until smooth. Fill paper cups with equal amounts of cherry mixture. Freeze several hours or until very slushy. Place popsicle sticks in the center of each cup. Freeze 1 hour longer or until firm. To serve, peel off paper cups.

Makes 8 servings

note: Serve immediately after peeling off paper cups—these pops melt very quickly.

Favorite recipe from **Cherry Marketing Institute**

helpful hint

If you're short on freezer space, try saving room by storing food in plastic freezer bags instead of rigid containers. Transfer cooled food to a bag, press out as much air as possible, seal the bag, lay it flat on a plate and place it in the freezer. Once the food is frozen solid, remove the plate and stack the bags.

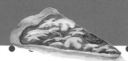

kids' quesadillas

Prep Time: 5 minutes • Cook Time: 15 minutes

8 slices American cheese
8 (10-inch) flour tortillas
½ pound thinly sliced deli turkey
6 tablespoons *French's*® Honey Mustard
2 tablespoons melted butter
¼ teaspoon paprika

1. To prepare 1 quesadilla, arrange 2 slices of cheese on 1 tortilla. Top with ¼ of the turkey. Spread with *1½ tablespoons* mustard, then top with another tortilla. Prepare 3 more quesadillas with remaining ingredients.

2. Combine butter and paprika. Brush one side of tortilla with butter mixture. Preheat 12-inch nonstick skillet over medium-high heat. Place tortilla butter side down and cook 2 minutes. Brush top of tortilla with butter mixture and turn over. Cook 1½ minutes or until golden brown. Repeat with remaining 3 quesadillas.

3. Slice into wedges before serving. *Makes 4 servings*

colorful kabobs

30 cocktail-size smoked sausages
10 to 20 cherry or grape tomatoes
10 to 20 large pimiento-stuffed green olives
2 yellow bell peppers, cut into 1-inch squares
1/4 cup (1/2 stick) butter or margarine, melted
    Lemon juice (optional)

1. Preheat oven to 450°F.

2. Thread 3 sausages onto 8-inch wooden skewer,* alternating with tomatoes, olives and bell peppers. Repeat on remaining nine skewers.

3. Place skewers on rack in shallow baking pan. Brush with melted butter and drizzle with lemon juice, if desired. Bake 4 to 6 minutes until hot.   *Makes 10 kabobs*

Soak skewers in water 20 minutes before using to prevent them from burning.

on-the-go guide: For younger children, remove food from skewers and serve in a paper cup or bowl. It's still portable, but much safer.

warm peanut-caramel dip

1/4 cup reduced-fat peanut butter
2 tablespoons fat-free caramel ice cream topping
2 tablespoons fat-free (skim) milk
1 large apple, cored and thinly sliced
4 large pretzel rods, broken in half

Combine peanut butter, caramel topping and milk in small saucepan. Heat over low heat, stirring constantly, until mixture is melted and warm. Serve with apple slices and pretzel rods.   *Makes 4 servings*

microwave directions: Combine all ingredients except apple and pretzel rods in small microwavable dish. Microwave on MEDIUM (50%) 1 minute; stir well. Microwave 1 minute more or until mixture is melted and warm.

HERSHEY®S easy chocolate cracker snacks

1²/₃ cups (10-ounce package) HERSHEY®S Mint Chocolate Chips*
2 cups (12-ounce package) HERSHEY®S Semi-Sweet Chocolate Chips
2 tablespoons shortening (do not use butter, margarine, spread or oil)
60 to 70 round buttery crackers (about one-half 1-pound box)

*2 cups (11.5-ounce package) HERSHEY®S Milk Chocolate Chips and ¼ teaspoon pure peppermint extract can be substituted for mint chocolate chips.

1. Line several trays or cookie sheets with wax paper.

2. Place mint chocolate chips, chocolate chips and shortening in large microwave-safe bowl. Microwave at HIGH (100%) 1 minute; stir. Continue heating 30 seconds at a time, stirring after each heating, until chips are melted and mixture is smooth when stirred.

3. Drop crackers into chocolate mixture one at a time. Using tongs, push cracker into chocolate so that it is covered completely. (If chocolate begins to thicken, reheat 10 to 20 seconds in microwave.) Remove from chocolate, tapping lightly on edge of bowl to remove excess chocolate. Place on prepared tray. Refrigerate until chocolate hardens, about 20 minutes. For best results, store tightly covered in refrigerator. *Makes about 5¹/₂ dozen crackers*

peanut butter and milk chocolate: Use 1²/₃ cups (10-ounce package) REESE'S® Peanut Butter Chips, 2 cups (11.5-ounce package) HERSHEY®S Milk Chocolate Chips and 2 tablespoons shortening. Proceed as directed.

white chip and toffee: Melt 2 bags (12 ounces each) HERSHEY®S Premier White Chips and 2 tablespoons shortening. Dip crackers; before coating hardens sprinkle with HEATH® BITS 'O BRICKLE® Toffee Bits.

jerk "dino" strips

¼ **cup reduced-fat mayonnaise**

2 **tablespoons orange marmalade or orange fruit spread**

1 **tablespoon fresh lime juice**

1 **teaspoon sugar**

¼ **teaspoon salt**

¼ **teaspoon ground ginger**

¼ **teaspoon garlic salt**

¼ **teaspoon black pepper**

⅛ **teaspoon ground red pepper**

1 **pound boneless chicken breast strips**

1. Preheat grill. Combine mayonnaise and orange marmalade in small bowl; set aside.

2. Combine lime juice, sugar, salt, ginger, garlic salt, black pepper and red pepper in shallow bowl. Roll chicken strips in seasoning mixture. Set aside 5 minutes to absorb seasonings.

3. Place chicken strips in grill basket over hot grid. Grill 3 to 4 minutes per side or until cooked through. Serve chicken strips with orange dip. *Makes 4 servings*

variation: If desired, broil chicken instead. Place on rack of broiler pan and broil 5 inches from heat 4 minutes per side or until cooked through.

breakfast mice

2 hard-cooked eggs, peeled and halved
2 teaspoons mayonnaise
¼ teaspoon salt
2 radishes, thinly sliced and root ends reserved
8 raisins or currants
1 ounce Cheddar cheese, shredded or cubed
Spinach leaves (optional)

1. Gently scoop egg yolks into small bowl. Mash yolks, mayonnaise and salt until smooth. Spoon yolk mixture back into egg halves. Place 2 halves, cut side down, on each serving plate.

2. Cut two tiny slits near the narrow end of each egg half; position 2 radish slices on each half for ears. Use the root end of each radish to form tails. Push raisins into each egg half to form eyes. Place small pile of cheese in front of each mouse. Garnish with spinach leaves, if desired.

Makes 2 servings

helpful hint

This surefire method to hard cook eggs comes from the American Egg Board. Place the eggs in a single layer in a saucepan. Add enough water to come at least 1 inch above the eggs. Cover and quickly bring water just to a boil. Turn off heat. If necessary, remove the pan from the burner to prevent further boiling. Let eggs stand, covered, in the hot water 15 to 17 minutes. Immediately run cold water over eggs or put them in ice water until completely cooled.

"here's looking at you, kid" chicken salad

2 large cucumbers (about 12 ounces each)
1 (5-ounce) can chicken breast meat, drained
3 tablespoons mayonnaise
   Olive slices and red bell pepper pieces

1. Peel and cut cucumbers into 16 rounds (about 1½ inches thick). Hollow out halfway through centers of cucumbers with spoon to make cups; set aside.

2. Mix chicken and mayonnaise in small bowl. Stir until well blended.

3. Stuff each cucumber cup with 1 heaping teaspoon chicken mixture.

4. Decorate with olive pieces to make eyes and smiles; use bell pepper pieces for noses.   *Makes 16 servings*

helpful hint

Try this recipe with tuna or ham salad, or use a zucchini in place of a cucumber. You can create faces from pieces of almost any vegetable. Get the kids involved in decorating and offer them an assortment of bell pepper strips, green onions, fresh herbs, or whatever they like and you have on hand.

funny-face cheese ball

Prep Time: 15 minutes

  2 packages (8 ounces each) reduced-fat cream cheese, softened
  2 cups (8 ounces) shredded Mexican cheese blend
1¼ cups shredded carrots, divided
  2 tablespoons fat-free (skim) milk
  2 teaspoons chili powder
  ¼ teaspoon ground cumin
  ¼ teaspoon garlic powder
  1 pimento-stuffed olive, sliced
  1 peperoncini pepper
    Red or yellow bell pepper pieces
    Reduced-fat shredded wheat crackers or celery sticks

1. Beat cream cheese, shredded cheese, 1 cup shredded carrots, milk, chili powder, cumin and garlic powder in large bowl with electric mixer at medium speed until well blended.

2. Shape mixture into ball. Arrange remaining ¼ cup shredded carrot on top of ball for hair. Use olive slices for eyes, peperoncini pepper for nose and bell pepper for ears and mouth.

3. Serve immediately or cover and refrigerate until serving time. Serve with crackers or celery sticks. *Makes 24 servings*

Crunch A Bunch

easy nachos

　　4 (6-inch) flour tortillas
　　　Nonstick cooking spray
　　4 ounces lean ground turkey
　　$^2/_3$ cup salsa (mild or medium)
　　2 tablespoons sliced green onion
　　$^1/_2$ cup (2 ounces) shredded reduced-fat Cheddar cheese

1. Preheat oven to 350°F. Cut each tortilla into 8 wedges; lightly spray one side of wedges with cooking spray. Place on ungreased baking sheet. Bake 5 to 9 minutes or until lightly browned and crisp.

2. Meanwhile, cook ground turkey in small nonstick skillet until browned, stirring with spoon to break up meat. Drain fat. Stir in salsa; cook until hot.

3. Sprinkle turkey mixture over tortilla wedges. Sprinkle with green onion. Top with cheese. Return to oven 1 to 2 minutes or until cheese melts.

Makes 4 servings

serving suggestion: Cut tortillas into shapes with cookie cutters and bake as directed.

tip: In a hurry? Substitute baked corn chips for flour tortillas and cooking spray. Proceed as directed.

crunchy comets

1 package (8 ounces) cream cheese, softened
1 egg yolk
$\frac{1}{3}$ cup granulated sugar
1 tablespoon all-purpose flour
1 teaspoon vanilla
$\frac{1}{2}$ teaspoon almond extract
1 package (16 ounces) phyllo dough, thawed
1 cup (2 sticks) butter, melted and cooled
1 can (21 ounces) cherry pie filling
Powdered sugar
Colored sugar

1. Preheat oven to 375°F. Beat cream cheese, egg yolk, sugar, flour, vanilla and almond extract in medium bowl until smooth. Chill about 30 minutes.

2. Unroll thawed phyllo dough; cover with plastic wrap and damp, clean kitchen towel to prevent drying out. Carefully remove single sheet and place on waxed paper. (Immediately recover remaining phyllo.) Brush sheet with melted butter. Fold in half; place 1 tablespoon cream cheese filling 3 inches from corner. Top with 1 or 2 drained cherries from pie filling. Turn corner of dough over filling, brush edges with butter and fold in sides to secure. Roll to completely enclose filling; gently twist dough into tail shape. Repeat with remaining filling and phyllo. Reserve extra pie filling.

3. Make a 3-inch thick roll of crumpled aluminum foil; place lengthwise on cookie sheet. Carefully lay twisted ends of phyllo over foil, bending slightly to form curved comet tails. Brush with melted butter and bake 12 to 15 minutes or until golden brown. Dust with powdered and colored sugars. Serve comets with reserved cherry pie filling.   *Makes 12 to 14 servings*

cracker toffee

72 **rectangular butter-flavored crackers**
1 **cup (2 sticks) unsalted butter**
1 **cup packed brown sugar**
¼ **teaspoon salt**
2½ **cups semisweet chocolate chips**
2 **cups chopped pecans**

1. Preheat oven to 375°F. Line 17×12-inch jelly-roll pan with heavy-duty foil. Spray generously with nonstick cooking spray. Arrange crackers with edges touching in pan; set aside.

2. Combine butter, brown sugar and salt in heavy medium saucepan. Heat over medium heat until butter melts, stirring frequently. Increase heat to high; boil 3 minutes without stirring. Pour mixture evenly over crackers; spread to cover.

3. Bake 5 minutes. Immediately sprinkle chocolate chips evenly over crackers; spread to cover. Sprinkle pecans over chocolate, pressing down. Cool to room temperature. Refrigerate 2 hours. Break into chunks to serve. *Makes 24 servings*

variation: Substitute peanut butter chips for chocolate chips and coarsely chopped, lightly salted peanuts for chopped pecans.

helpful hint

All chocolate should be stored, tightly wrapped, in a cool, dry place. The greyish blotches, called "bloom," that sometimes appear on chocolate are caused by cocoa butter rising to the surface when the chocolate gets too warm. It is still safe to use, but the flavor will be slightly compromised.

cinnamon toast poppers

2 tablespoons butter
6 cups fresh bread* cubes (1-inch cubes)
1 tablespoon plus 1½ teaspoons sugar
½ teaspoon ground cinnamon

*Use a firm sourdough, whole wheat or semolina bread.

1. Preheat oven to 325°F. Melt butter in Dutch oven or large skillet over low heat. Add bread cubes and toss to coat; remove from heat. Combine sugar and cinnamon in small bowl. Sprinkle over bread cubes; stir well.

2. Spread bread cubes in one layer on ungreased baking sheet. Bake 25 minutes or until bread is golden and fragrant, stirring once or twice. Serve warm or at room temperature. *Makes 12 servings*

popcorn truffles

8 cups popped plain popcorn
2 cups (12 ounces) semisweet chocolate chips
   Colored sprinkles (optional)

1. Line 2 baking sheets with waxed paper. Place popcorn in large bowl.

2. Place chocolate chips in microwavable bowl. Microwave on HIGH 30 seconds; stir. Repeat, if necessary, until chips are melted. Pour over popcorn; stir until well coated.

3. Scoop popcorn mixture with small ice cream scoop, pressing mixture slightly against the inside of bowl. Drop by scoopfuls onto prepared baking sheets. Decorate with sprinkles, if desired. Allow to harden at room temperature or refrigerate. Store truffles in air-tight container up to 3 days. *Makes 40 (1½-inch) truffles*

cranberry gorp

¼ cup (½ stick) butter
¼ cup packed light brown sugar
1 tablespoon maple syrup
1 teaspoon curry powder
½ teaspoon ground cinnamon
1½ cups dried cranberries
1½ cups coarsely chopped walnuts and/or slivered almonds
1½ cups lightly salted pretzel nuggets

1. Preheat oven to 300°F. Grease 15×10-inch jelly-roll pan. Combine butter, brown sugar and maple syrup in large saucepan; heat over medium heat until butter is melted. Stir in curry powder and cinnamon. Add cranberries, walnuts and pretzels; stir until well blended.

2. Spread mixture on prepared pan. Bake 15 minutes or until mixture is crunchy and light brown. *Makes 20 servings*

crunchy turkey pita pockets

1 cup diced cooked boneless skinless turkey breast or chicken breast
½ cup packaged coleslaw mix
½ cup dried cranberries
¼ cup shredded carrot
2 tablespoons reduced-fat mayonnaise
1 tablespoon honey mustard
2 (6-inch) rounds whole wheat pita bread, cut in half

1. Combine turkey, coleslaw mix, cranberries, carrots, mayonnaise and mustard in small bowl; mix well.

2. Fill pitas with turkey mixture. *Makes 2 servings*

coconut honey popcorn balls

3 quarts popped JOLLY TIME® Pop Corn
³/₄ cup coconut
¹/₃ cup honey
¹/₂ teaspoon ground cinnamon
Dash of salt
3 tablespoons butter or margarine

Preheat oven to 250°F. Line shallow pan with foil. Place popped popcorn in pan. Keep popcorn warm in oven. Spread coconut in shallow baking pan; toast coconut in oven, stirring once, about 8 to 10 minutes. Combine honey, cinnamon and salt in small saucepan. Heat to boiling; boil 2¹/₂ minutes, stirring constantly. Add butter; stir until melted. Pour honey mixture over popcorn. Add coconut. Toss well. Cool just enough to handle. With JOLLY TIME® Pop Corn Ball Maker or buttered hands, shape into balls.

Makes about 10 popcorn balls

chocolate almond cherry mix

2 cups toasted almonds*
2 cups candy-coated chocolate pieces
2 cups dried cherries

*To toast almonds, spread nuts in a shallow baking pan. Bake in preheated 350°F oven 10 to 15 minutes, stirring occasionally.

Combine all ingredients in large bowl; mix well.   *Makes 6 cups*

pretzel fried eggs

24 pretzel rings (1-inch)
1 cup white chocolate chips
24 yellow candy-coated chocolate pieces

1. Line baking sheet with waxed paper. Place pretzel rings on prepared backing sheet about 2 inches apart.

2. Place white chocolate chips in 1-quart resealable food storage bag; seal bag. Microwave on HIGH 30 seconds. Knead bag gently and microwave 30 seconds more; repeat until chips are melted. Cut 1/4-inch corner from bag.

3. Squeeze chocolate from bag onto each pretzel ring in circular motion. Fill center of pretzel first and finish with ring of chocolate around edge of pretzel. Use tip of small knife to smooth chocolate, if necessary. Place candy piece in center of each pretzel. Allow to harden at room temperature or refrigerate until set. Store in single layer in air-tight container up to one week.   *Makes 24 eggs*

variation: To make "green eggs and ham," use green candy-coated chocolate pieces for yolks. Cut small pieces of pink fruit leather for ham. Serve 2 Pretzel Fried Eggs with small strips of fruit leather bacon and square cinnamon cereal for toast.

crispy cookie treats

1 package (18 ounces) refrigerated miniature chocolate chip
    cookie dough (40 count)
1/2 cup (1 stick) butter
1/2 teaspoon ground cinnamon
1 package (16 ounces) miniature marshmallows
4 cups crisp rice cereal
2 cups unsweetened granola

1. Bake cookies according to package directions. Reserve 24 cooled cookies. Coarsely chop remaining 16 cookies. Place chopped cookies in resealable food storage bag; seal bag. Freeze at least 1 hour.

2. Melt butter in large saucepan over medium heat; stir in cinnamon. Add marshmallows; cook and stir until melted and smooth. Remove from heat; let stand 10 minutes, stirring every few minutes.

3. Meanwhile, lightly grease 13×9-inch baking pan and rubber spatula. Combine cereal, granola and frozen chopped cookies in large bowl. Pour marshmallow mixture over cereal mixture; stir with spatula until well blended.

4. Press mixture into prepared pan; flatten with lightly greased waxed paper or hands. Press reserved 24 cookies on top of bars, spacing evenly. Let stand at room temperature about 2 hours or until set. Cut into 2×2¼-inch bars.   *Makes 2 dozen bars*

spicy fruity popcorn mix

4 cups lightly salted popped popcorn
2 cups corn cereal squares
1½ cups dried pineapple wedges
1 package (6 ounces) dried fruit bits
   Butter-flavored cooking spray
2 tablespoons sugar
1 tablespoon ground cinnamon
1 cup yogurt-covered raisins

1. Preheat oven to 350°F. Combine popcorn, cereal, pineapple and fruit bits in large bowl; mix lightly. Transfer to 15×10-inch jelly-roll pan. Spray mixture generously with cooking spray.

2. Combine sugar and cinnamon in small bowl. Sprinkle half of sugar mixture over popcorn mixture; toss lightly to coat. Spray mixture again with additional cooking spray. Add remaining sugar mixture; mix lightly.

3. Bake 10 minutes, stirring after 5 minutes. Cool completely in pan on wire rack. Add raisins; mix lightly.

Makes about 8½ cups snack mix

helpful hint

Snack mixes are easy to put together and making them yourself allows you to choose only the ingredients your family likes. You can make a healthier treat than most of the ready-made mixes, too. A sandwich bag filled with homemade snack mix is the perfect addition to any lunch box.

cinnamon apple chips

2 cups unsweetened apple juice
1 cinnamon stick
2 Washington Red Delicious apples

1. In large skillet or saucepan, combine apple juice and cinnamon stick; bring to a low boil while preparing apples.

2. With paring knife, slice off ½ inch from tops and bottoms of apples and discard (or eat). Stand apples on either cut end; cut crosswise into ⅛-inch-thick slices, rotating apple as necessary to cut even slices.

3. Drop slices into boiling juice; cook 4 to 5 minutes or until slices appear translucent and lightly golden. Meanwhile, preheat oven to 250°F.

4. With slotted spatula, remove apple slices from juice and pat dry. Arrange slices on wire racks, making sure none overlap. Place racks on middle shelf in oven; bake 30 to 40 minutes until slices are lightly browned and almost dry to touch. Let chips cool on racks completely before storing in airtight container.   *Makes about 40 chips*

tip: There is no need to core apples because boiling in juice for several minutes softens core and removes seeds.

Favorite recipe from **Washington Apple Commission**

Sweet Stuff

banana split ice cream sandwiches

- 1 package (18 ounces) refrigerated chocolate chip cookie dough
- 2 ripe bananas, mashed
- $\frac{1}{2}$ cup strawberry jam, divided
- 4 cups strawberry ice cream (or any flavor), softened
  Hot fudge topping and whipped cream (optional)
- 9 maraschino cherries (optional)

1. Preheat oven to 350°F. Lightly grease 13×9-inch baking pan. Let dough stand at room temperature about 15 minutes.

2. Combine dough and bananas in large bowl; beat until well blended. Spread dough evenly in prepared pan; smooth top. Bake about 22 minutes or until edges are light brown. Cool completely in pan on wire rack.

3. Line 8×8-inch baking pan with aluminum foil or plastic wrap, allowing some to hang over edges of pan. Remove cooled cookie from pan; cut in half crosswise. Place 1 cookie half, top side down, in prepared pan, trimming edges to fit, if necessary. Spread ¼ cup jam evenly over cookie in pan. Spread ice cream evenly over jam. Spread remaining ¼ cup jam over bottom of remaining cookie half; place jam side down on ice cream. Cover tightly with foil or plastic wrap; freeze at least 2 hours or overnight.

4. Cut into bars and top with hot fudge sauce, whipped cream and cherries, if desired.
Makes 9 servings

snickerpoodles

1 package (18 ounces) refrigerated sugar cookie dough
1 teaspoon ground cinnamon, divided
1 teaspoon vanilla
¼ cup sugar
   Chocolate chips and mini chocolate chips
   Prepared white icing (optional)

1. Preheat oven to 350°F. Lightly grease cookie sheets. Let dough stand at room temperature about 15 minutes.

2. Combine dough, ½ teaspoon cinnamon and vanilla in large bowl; beat until well blended. Combine sugar and remaining ½ teaspoon cinnamon in small bowl. For each poodle face, shape ½ tablespoon dough into oval. Roll in cinnamon-sugar; place on prepared cookie sheet. For poodle ears, divide ½ tablespoon dough in half; shape each half into teardrop shape. Roll in cinnamon-sugar; place on cookie sheet at either side of face. For top of poodle head, shape scant teaspoon dough into oval. Roll in cinnamon-sugar; place on cookie sheet at top of face.

3. Bake 10 to 12 minutes or until edges are lightly browned. Immediately press 1 chocolate chip and 2 mini chocolate chips upside down in face for nose and eyes. Cool 2 minutes on cookie sheets. Remove to wire racks; cool completely.

4. Decorate with icing, if desired.   *Makes about 2 dozen cookies*

frozen florida monkey malt

Prep Time: 5 minutes

2 bananas, peeled
1 cup milk
5 tablespoons frozen orange juice concentrate
3 tablespoons malted milk powder

1. Wrap bananas in plastic wrap; freeze.

2. Break bananas into pieces; place in blender with milk, orange juice concentrate and malted milk powder. Blend until smooth; pour into glasses to serve. *Makes 2 servings*

chocolate-dipped strawberries

2 cups (11½ ounces) milk chocolate chips
1 tablespoon shortening
12 large strawberries with stems, rinsed and dried

1. Line baking sheet with waxed paper; set aside.

2. Melt chips with shortening in top of double boiler over hot, not boiling, water, stirring constantly.

3. Dip about half of each strawberry in chocolate. Remove excess chocolate by scraping bottom of strawberry across rim of pan. Place strawberries on prepared baking sheet. Let stand until set.

4. Store in refrigerator in container between layers of waxed paper.
Makes about 12 strawberries

variation: Melt 8 ounces white chocolate or pastel confectionery coating. Dip chocolate-dipped strawberries into white chocolate leaving a portion of the milk chocolate coating showing.

hint: Stir chopped dried fruits, raisins or nuts into remaining chocolate; drop by tablespoonfuls onto a baking sheet lined with waxed paper.

s'more cups

1 package (18 ounces) refrigerated miniature chocolate chip cookie dough
1 cup graham cracker crumbs
1²/₃ cups semisweet chocolate chips
1 cup (¹/₂ pint) whipping cream
1 package (10 ounces) miniature marshmallows
18 bear-shaped graham crackers

1. Preheat oven to 350°F. Lightly grease 18 standard (2¹/₂-inch) muffin cups or line with paper baking cups. Let dough stand at room temperature about 15 minutes.

2. Combine dough and cracker crumbs in large bowl; beat until well blended. Shape dough into 18 balls; press onto bottoms and up sides of prepared muffin cups.

3. Bake 12 to 15 minutes or until set. Remove from oven; gently press down center of each cookie cup with back of teaspoon. Cool in pans 10 minutes. Remove cups from pans; cool completely on wire rack.

4. Place chocolate chips in large bowl. Place cream in small saucepan; bring to a boil over medium heat. Pour hot cream over chocolate chips; stir until chocolate is melted and mixture is smooth. Cool 5 minutes. Meanwhile, preheat broiler.

5. Place cookie cups on ungreased cookie sheet. Divide cooled chocolate mixture evenly among cookie cups. Place 7 marshmallows on top of each cup. Broil cookie cups 20 to 30 seconds or until marshmallows are golden brown. Top with bear-shaped graham crackers. *Makes 1¹/₂ dozen cups*

peanut butter fudge brownie bars

1 cup (2 sticks) butter or margarine, melted
1½ cups sugar
2 eggs
1 teaspoon vanilla extract
1¼ cups all-purpose flour
⅔ cup HERSHEY'S Cocoa
¼ cup milk
1¼ cups chopped pecans or walnuts, divided
½ cup (1 stick) butter or margarine
1⅔ cups (10-ounce package) REESE'S® Peanut Butter Chips
1 can (14 ounces) sweetened condensed milk (not evaporated milk)
¼ cup HERSHEY'S Semi-Sweet Chocolate Chips

1. Heat oven to 350°F. Grease 13×9×2-inch baking pan.

2. Beat melted butter, sugar, eggs and vanilla in large bowl with electric mixer on medium speed until well blended. Add flour, cocoa and milk; beat until blended. Stir in 1 cup nuts. Spread in prepared pan.

3. Bake 25 to 30 minutes or just until edges begin to pull away from sides of pan. Cool completely in pan on wire rack.

4. Melt ½ cup butter and peanut butter chips in medium saucepan over low heat, stirring constantly. Add sweetened condensed milk, stirring until smooth; pour over baked layer.

5. Place chocolate chips in small microwave-safe bowl. Microwave at HIGH (100%) 45 seconds or just until chips are melted when stirred. Drizzle bars with melted chocolate; sprinkle with remaining ¼ cup nuts. Refrigerate 1 hour or until firm. Cut into bars. Cover; refrigerate leftover bars. *Makes 36 bars*

miss pinky the pig cupcakes

    2 jars (10 ounces each) maraschino cherries, well drained
    1 package white cake mix *without* pudding in the mix
    1 cup sour cream
    ½ cup vegetable oil
    3 egg whites
    ¼ cup water
    ½ teaspoon almond extract
      Red food coloring
    1 container (16 ounces) cream cheese frosting
   48 small gumdrops
      Mini candy coated chocolate pieces, chocolate chips,
        white decorating icing and colored sugar

1. Preheat oven to 350°F. Line 24 standard (2½-inch) muffin cups with paper baking cups. Spray 24 mini (1¾-inch) muffin cups with nonstick cooking spray. Pat cherries dry with paper towels. Place in food processor; process 4 to 5 seconds or until finely chopped.

2. Beat cake mix, sour cream, oil, egg whites, water and almond extract in large bowl with electric mixer at low speed about 1 minute or until blended. Increase speed to medium; beat 1 to 2 minutes or until smooth. Stir in cherries.

3. Spoon 2 slightly rounded tablespoons batter into each prepared standard muffin cup, filling about half full. Spoon remaining batter into prepared mini muffin cups, filling about one-third full.

4. Bake standard cupcakes 14 to 18 minutes and mini cupcakes 7 to 9 minutes or until toothpick inserted into centers comes out clean. Cool cupcakes in pans on wire racks 5 minutes. Remove to wire racks; cool completely.

5. Add food coloring to frosting, a few drops at a time, until desired shade of pink is reached. Frost tops of large cupcakes. Press top of small cupcake onto one side of each large cupcake top. Frost small cupcakes.

6. Place gumdrops between two layers of waxed paper. Flatten to $\frac{1}{8}$-inch thickness with rolling pin; cut out triangles. Arrange gumdrops on cupcakes for ears; complete faces with candy-coated chocolate pieces, chocolate chips, white icing and colored sugar.

Makes 24 cupcakes

rocky road brownies

$1\frac{1}{4}$ **cups miniature marshmallows**

1 **cup HERSHEY'S Semi-Sweet Chocolate Chips**

$\frac{1}{2}$ **cup chopped nuts**

$\frac{1}{2}$ **cup (1 stick) butter or margarine**

1 **cup sugar**

2 **eggs**

1 **teaspoon vanilla extract**

$\frac{1}{2}$ **cup all-purpose flour**

$\frac{1}{3}$ **cup HERSHEY'S Cocoa**

$\frac{1}{2}$ **teaspoon baking powder**

$\frac{1}{2}$ **teaspoon salt**

1. Heat oven to 350°F. Grease 9-inch square baking pan.

2. Stir together marshmallows, chocolate chips and nuts; set aside. Place butter in large microwave-safe bowl. Microwave at HIGH (100%) 1 to $1\frac{1}{2}$ minutes or until melted. Add sugar, eggs and vanilla, beating with spoon until well blended. Add flour, cocoa, baking powder and salt; blend well. Spread batter in prepared pan.

3. Bake 22 minutes. Sprinkle chocolate chip mixture over top. Continue baking 5 minutes or until marshmallows have softened and puffed slightly. Cool completely. With wet knife, cut into squares.

Makes about 20 brownies

frozen pudding cups

Prep Time: 10 minutes • Freeze Time: 3 hours

>   1 package (4-serving size) chocolate instant pudding and pie
>   filling mix
>   1 package (4-serving size) vanilla instant pudding and pie
>   filling mix
>   5 cups cold milk, divided
>   Fresh sliced strawberries

1. Whisk together chocolate pudding mix and 2$\frac{1}{2}$ cups milk in medium bowl about 2 minutes. Repeat with vanilla pudding mix and remaining 2$\frac{1}{2}$ cups milk in another medium bowl.

2. Divide half of chocolate pudding among 8 plastic cups. Layer half of vanilla pudding over chocolate. Repeat layers; cover with plastic wrap and freeze until firm, about 3 hours. Thaw pudding cups at room temperature 1 hour before serving. Top with sliced strawberries.

Makes 8 servings

chocolate-covered raisins

>   2 cups (11$\frac{1}{2}$ ounces) milk chocolate chips
>   1 square (1 ounce) unsweetened chocolate, chopped
>   1 tablespoon shortening
>   2 cups raisins

1. Line baking sheet with waxed paper; butter generously. Set aside.

2. Melt chips and chopped chocolate with shortening in medium saucepan over low heat, stirring constantly. Stir in raisins.

3. Drop individual raisins or drop in clusters from spoon onto prepared baking sheet. Let stand until firm.

Makes about 1$\frac{1}{2}$ pounds

banana split shakes

　1 small (6-inch) ripe banana
　¼ cup fat-free (skim) milk
　5 maraschino cherries, drained
　1 tablespoon chocolate syrup
　⅛ teaspoon coconut extract
　4 cups low-fat chocolate frozen yogurt

1. Combine banana, milk, cherries, chocolate syrup and coconut extract in blender. Cover; blend on HIGH speed until smooth.

2. Add yogurt 1 cup at a time; cover, and pulse on HIGH speed until smooth and thick. Pour into 4 glasses. Garnish with additional maraschino cherries, if desired. *Makes 4 servings*

tip: For a low-fat shake, chop 3 large peeled bananas. Place in resealable food storage bag and freeze until solid. (This is a great use for over-ripe bananas.) Blend with milk, cherries, chocolate syrup and coconut extract. It will not be as thick and frosty, but will be lower in calories and fat.

crunchy peppermint candy ice cream

　1¼ cups water
　1 (14-ounce) can EAGLE BRAND® Sweetened Condensed Milk
　　(NOT evaporated milk)
　2 cups (1 pint) light cream
　½ cup crushed hard peppermint candy
　1 tablespoon vanilla extract

1. Combine all ingredients in ice cream freezer container. Freeze according to manufacturer's instructions.

2. Garnish with additional crushed peppermint candy (optional). Freeze leftovers. *Makes 1½ quarts*

The publisher would like to thank the companies and organizations listed below for the use of their recipes and photographs in this publication.

Cherry Marketing Institute

EAGLE BRAND®

The Hershey Company

The Hidden Valley® Food Products Company

JOLLY TIME® Pop Corn

National Watermelon Promotion Board

Reckitt Benckiser Inc.

The Sugar Association, Inc.

Unilever

Washington Apple Commission

METRIC CONVERSION CHART

VOLUME MEASUREMENTS (dry)

$1/8$ teaspoon = 0.5 mL
$1/4$ teaspoon = 1 mL
$1/2$ teaspoon = 2 mL
$3/4$ teaspoon = 4 mL
1 teaspoon = 5 mL
1 tablespoon = 15 mL
2 tablespoons = 30 mL
$1/4$ cup = 60 mL
$1/3$ cup = 75 mL
$1/2$ cup = 125 mL
$2/3$ cup = 150 mL
$3/4$ cup = 175 mL
1 cup = 250 mL
2 cups = 1 pint = 500 mL
3 cups = 750 mL
4 cups = 1 quart = 1 L

VOLUME MEASUREMENTS (fluid)

1 fluid ounce (2 tablespoons) = 30 mL
4 fluid ounces ($1/2$ cup) = 125 mL
8 fluid ounces (1 cup) = 250 mL
12 fluid ounces ($1 1/2$ cups) = 375 mL
16 fluid ounces (2 cups) = 500 mL

WEIGHTS (mass)

$1/2$ ounce = 15 g
1 ounce = 30 g
3 ounces = 90 g
4 ounces = 120 g
8 ounces = 225 g
10 ounces = 285 g
12 ounces = 360 g
16 ounces = 1 pound = 450 g

DIMENSIONS

$1/16$ inch = 2 mm
$1/8$ inch = 3 mm
$1/4$ inch = 6 mm
$1/2$ inch = 1.5 cm
$3/4$ inch = 2 cm
1 inch = 2.5 cm

OVEN TEMPERATURES

250°F = 120°C
275°F = 140°C
300°F = 150°C
325°F = 160°C
350°F = 180°C
375°F = 190°C
400°F = 200°C
425°F = 220°C
450°F = 230°C

BAKING PAN SIZES

Utensil	Size in Inches/Quarts	Metric Volume	Size in Centimeters
Baking or Cake Pan (square or rectangular)	8×8×2	2 L	20×20×5
	9×9×2	2.5 L	23×23×5
	12×8×2	3 L	30×20×5
	13×9×2	3.5 L	33×23×5
Loaf Pan	8×4×3	1.5 L	20×10×7
	9×5×3	2 L	23×13×7
Round Layer Cake Pan	8×1½	1.2 L	20×4
	9×1½	1.5 L	23×4
Pie Plate	8×1¼	750 mL	20×3
	9×1¼	1 L	23×3
Baking Dish or Casserole	1 quart	1 L	—
	1½ quart	1.5 L	—
	2 quart	2 L	—